THE
TITLE
IS THE
PROBLEM

THE
TITLE
is the
PROBLEM

Why "Executive Assistant" Falls Short

Anne Browning

Orcheo Press

Published by Orcheo Press ISBN: 979-8-9930532-5-7

Cover design by Orcheo
Interior design by Orcheo
Edited by Orcheo
Printed in the United States of America

Dedication

To my parents,

Who planted courage in my bones and grace in my stride. Your quiet sacrifices are stitched into every page.

To my siblings,

The keepers of my roots and co-conspirators in resilience. You remind me of who I've always been.

To my dearest friends,

The ones who stayed, who saw, who stood beside me, you are the soul of my laughter and the shelter in every storm.

To the LinkedIn EA community,

A mosaic of brilliance, strength, and resilience. Your voices echoed in my heart and helped me find my own. This is for us.

To *that one leader*, yes, you.

Thank you for seeing beyond the surface, for showing me what partnership should look like.

To my son,

A man now, thoughtful, bold, becoming. You teach me every day what it means to evolve with grace. You are my deepest why.

And to my husband,

My home, my calm, my unwavering companion. In the noise, you were the stillness. In the doubt, you were the anchor. This book exists because your love holds the space for it to grow.

Author Bio

Anne Browning is a powerhouse Executive Assistant, strategic partner, and unapologetic advocate for the evolution of administrative leadership. With over two decades of experience supporting C-suite executives across healthcare, finance, and corporate sectors, Anne brings clarity, precision, and heart to every table she sits at.

Known for her unflinching honesty and her fierce belief in the value of support roles, Anne has made it her mission to elevate the voices behind the title, challenging outdated norms and redefining what it means to lead from beside.

Her writing and thought leadership, shared alongside a remarkable LinkedIn EA community, have sparked conversations that name the unseen labor, honor the brilliance behind the role, and remind the world that power doesn't always sit in the front of the room.

Anne is as much at home in the saddle as she is in the boardroom. A lifelong equestrian, from championing hunter jumper and equitation in her youth to Western riding and horsemanship today, she carries forward the lessons of trust and partnership that horses teach into every aspect of her work and life.

A Texan at heart, Anne chooses a life of simplicity, pours love fiercely into the people and passions that matter most, and greets each day with openness, humility, and wonder. This is her first book, but not her last.

Table of Contents

Introduction

This book began with a question I've asked myself too many times to count: *Why does the business rely on me as its infrastructure, yet reduce me to a footnote in title?*

Ever asked yourself that too?

I have, many times. For more than twenty years, I've sat at the side of senior leaders. I've guided focus, balanced execution, navigated uncertainty, and built trust that rarely makes it onto paper. And yet, the title I carried never seemed to match the depth of what I was doing.

Has your title ever felt incomplete too? Like it only tells the surface story of a role that goes much deeper than anyone sees?

If you're an Executive Assistant, you know exactly what I'm talking about. But before you think this book is only for EAs, let me stop you, because it's not.

This is for every administrative professional: office managers, chiefs of staff, coordinators, project administrators. It's for anyone who carries tremendous value and responsibility without ever receiving the recognition to match.

And when I say recognition:

- I don't mean a pat on the back or a thank-you card.
- I mean authority.
- I mean credibility.
- I mean compensation.

The same tangible, measurable rewards we build into every other career path. Administrative work deserves to be monetized and legitimized just as much as any other profession.

You've felt the disconnect, haven't you? Between your title and your scope. You've been asked to stretch, absorb, lead, and perform, all without the clarity, authority, or compensation that usually comes with that level of contribution.

That's why I authored this book.

Because it must change.

Now, let me tell you what this book is not.

It is not a memoir.

It is not a training manual.

It is a conversation between me and you. One grounded in lived experience, shaped by hard truths, and fueled by a refusal to let the administrative profession keep being minimized in modern leadership.

Think about it.

- How many times have you been told to "stay in your lane," while in the same breath being asked to build the road?
- How many times have you led from behind, beside, or even ahead, without acknowledgment?
- How many times has your organization said they value staff, yet failed to truly define what support looks like in today's world?

That is what we are going to unpack together.

We are going to challenge outdated definitions, call out systemic misalignment, and hold up a mirror to the quiet cost of undervaluing those who keep everything moving.

But more than that, this is a reclamation.

- Of our worth.
- Our voice.
- And our right to be seen, not just as support, but as partners in leadership.

Ready?
Let's get to work.

Chapter 1: A Position Next to Power, Not Below It

I once took 20 minutes to pull the white M&Ms from a bowl filled with red, white, and blue M&Ms.

Why? Because the CEO didn't like how they looked.

In that moment, I didn't hesitate. I was inexperienced, driven, and keen to demonstrate my value. I believed this was simply what it meant to be an outstanding Executive Assistant: remain alert, be supportive, and become irreplaceable.

I now recognize that moment for what it truly was: a glimpse into how effortlessly this role can be misunderstood, misapplied, and overlooked.

Throughout the years, I've been referred to as an air-traffic controller (which I dislike the most), a scheduler, a problem-solver, and even once as "the one who brings the good pens." While these labels may seem endearing, they oversimplify my role. They indicate a superficial grasp of a position that functions much deeper than what is apparent.

The term "assistant" comes from the Latin word assistere, which translates to "to stand by." Traditionally, this has led to administrative professional positions viewed as passive, subordinate, and focused on tasks.

I am, like many Executive Assistants, the operational core of an organization. We are not "just" anything.

We are time strategists.

- We are decision accelerators.
- We are the temperature gauges of "the mood."
- We are energy protectors.
- We are the ones tracking the second- and third- order effects of today's choices on next month's outcomes.

We manage the spaces our leaders move through, so they can lead without friction. But that doesn't fit neatly into a title. And too often, it's not seen at all.

I was no longer just overseeing a calendar; I was overseeing the rhythm of our work. Each meeting I arranged carried strategic importance. Every agenda I crafted served as a roadmap for decisions. I wasn't merely coordinating logistics; I was turning vision into action.

I started sitting in executive meetings. Not as a notetaker, but as a second brain. I filtered noise, connected dots, and cleared obstacles before they were even visible. I bridged gaps between departments. I served as a backchannel for truth when hierarchy created silence. I earned trust quietly and operated boldly.

I turned ambiguity into action.

I made sure the right people had the right conversations at the right time. I anticipated, adjusted, and executed repeatedly.

But my title didn't change, despite my expanding role. It failed to represent the connections I nurtured, the frameworks I upheld, or the momentum I safeguarded.

And I'm not the exception. Thousands of highly skilled professionals are still working under a title that signals task, not impact.

Just to clarify. This isn't about pride. It's about accuracy.

When the scope and title are misaligned, the effects are significant: Value diminishes. Compensation falls behind. Access diminishes. Growth comes to a halt.

Now imagine if we applied this mismatch elsewhere.

Imagine calling a CFO "the budget person." Or a COO "the one who makes sure stuff runs."

Technically true. But wildly incomplete.

Their titles carry weight. They signal trust, strategic oversight, and decision-making authority.

For Executive Assistants, professionals who coordinate priorities, protect energy, and keep momentum alive, we still use a title anchored in the 1950s.

A title that implies subordination. A title that signals task over trust. A title that hides scale behind service.

And it shows.

A few months back, I was called a "secretary." Not by someone who didn't understand the role, but by a colleague from another department. It wasn't intended as an insult; it was casual. Dismissive. Lazy.

Right after calling me "the secretary," they handed me a printout like it was just part of the job—because that's what they assume admin roles are for.

Never mind that I was in the middle of structuring a cross-functional strategy session that touched five departments. Never mind that it would've been faster and more efficient for them to print it. The assumption was baked in.

That kind of assumption, born from outdated titles, distorts not just perception, but performance.

Here's the hidden cost of misunderstanding the role: Everyone loses. Leaders lose time. Teams lose clarity. Organizations lose momentum. You undercut the entire leadership infrastructure EAs uphold.

Here's how that plays out in real time:

- The executive doesn't loop the EA into early-stage discussions, so critical context is missing when it's time to execute.
- The EA isn't invited into high-level meetings, so misalignment grows between what's discussed and what's done.
- Projects stall, communication breaks down, and friction builds, all because the EA was viewed as a "doer" instead of a partner.
- A new executive inherits a legacy EA and assumes they are entry level when in fact, they've been the unofficial Chief of Staff for years.

Then... one of the most foreseeable and harmful patterns emerges. The EA departs.

Section 1: When the EA Leaves

When an Executive Assistant departs, most people assume it's no big deal.

"Just move a few tasks around. The other EAs can absorb it. It's all admin work, right?"

Wrong.

What happens is a dump, not a transition. Their workload gets scattered across already maxed-out EAs and coordinators who have no context, no bandwidth, and no support. Why? Because the assumption is that the work was lightweight.

Invisible. Easy.

What's really gone?

- The judgment calls that protected executive time.
- The shorthand communication that saved hours each week.
- The proactive calendar choreography that kept priorities aligned.
- The calm presence in chaos who knew what not to say, when to push, and when to pause.

Leadership underestimates the scope. Instead of replacing it strategically, they divide and conquer: one person gets the inbox, another the travel, and the rest disappears into the ether.

It often takes two or three people, sometimes more, to even begin to cover the void. Not because the EA was doing too much... But because what they were doing was complex, high-trust, and essential.

- You don't just lose a scheduler.
- You lose an orchestrator.

- You lose someone who moved decisions forward behind the scenes.
- Who saw around corners.
- Who knew where the landmines were buried and how to walk the team around them, without ever drawing attention to it.

Section 2: Misunderstood. Underutilized. Overlooked.

When you misunderstand the EA role, you don't just underutilize a person, you undercut the entire leadership infrastructure they uphold. Projects stall. Communication fractures. Strategic rhythm is lost. Everyone loses.

Leaders often experience burnout at a much quicker rate. As a result, systems begin to slow down significantly. Consequently, the organization starts to lose both its velocity and its focus.

And the most concerning aspect of this situation? It is entirely preventable if addressed in a timely manner.

Because when you take the time to see Executive Assistants for whom they truly are; strategic partners, execution engines, and vital culture carriers, you unlock not just essential support, but a wealth of untapped potential that can transform your organization.

You unlock significant impact.

Real, transformative impact. Not from a seat that is merely beneath power.

But from a seat that is positioned right beside it, actively engaging and influencing.

Chapter 2: If My Title Matched My Workload…

Section 1 - The Problem: Titles Shape Perception, Compensation, and Opportunity

I have heard repeatedly from leaders that titles are not important to them, and I understand the place where that comes from. But we do not talk enough about how much a title shapes perception until it is working against you.

For Executive Assistants, that moment comes early and often.

You introduce yourself at a networking event or in a meeting with external stakeholders. You say, "I am the Executive Assistant to the CEO."

And just like that, the temperature shifts. The interest fades. The assumptions rush in. The dynamic tilts. You can feel your credibility recalibrated, marginalized, in real time.

Even with the expertise, the breadth of responsibilities, the impact, and the significant operational role, the term Executive Assistant still evokes outdated perceptions: someone who simply arranges travel, manages calendars, takes notes, and handles a variety of tasks.

Forget that you just outlined the complete Q4 budget strategy implementation. Never mind that you are the connective tissue between eight departments. The title reads "assistant," which implies task manager to the world.

This goes beyond mere word choice.

Titles do more than describe. They convey meaning. They define how others engage with you, how leaders delegate to you, and how organizations choose to value or devalue your contribution.

When you refer to someone as a "Project Manager," people think of deliverables, deadlines, and dashboards. A "Chief of Staff" implies strategy, confidentiality, and close access to executives. But when you refer to someone as an "Executive Assistant," even those with good intentions often default to: Can you reserve the meeting space?

The significance of the work is not the issue. The problem is that the title has not evolved with the actual responsibilities and impact.

The result? A drag on perception. A drag on compensation. A drag on opportunity.

Yes, compensation must be equal to contribution. And for a vast number of high-functioning EAs, this is not the reality. Because here is the truth no one wants to say aloud: "Assistant" is no longer a descriptor. It is a distortion.

For high-functioning executive support, the title is not just outdated. It is a constraint.

Section 2 - The Misalignment: Same Title, Wildly Different Roles

If you have ever found it difficult to describe your job, you are not alone. It is not because you lack clarity. It is because the terminology we use is outdated and, quite frankly, incorrect.

You are part strategist, part operator, and part diplomat. Each day, you manage bandwidth, risk, communication, and execution. Yet try to condense that into a single line under a title like Executive Assistant, and you will notice how quickly people lose interest.

It is not a lack of value. It is a lack of language.

Unlike every other profession, EAs are boxed into one umbrella title that covers the entire spectrum, from entry-level transactional support to strategic partnership at the highest levels of leadership. That is a design flaw.

Other industries evolved their titles with their work:

- We have "People Partners" instead of HR Generalists.
- We have "Product Owners" instead of Product Coordinators.
- We have "Revenue Enablement" instead of Sales Support.

Meanwhile, EAs have quietly taken on more responsibility, complexity, and leadership-facing work than ever before, while still being referred to in language that predates modern business infrastructure.

And it shows up everywhere:

- Job descriptions that list "scheduling" and "duties as assigned" while the actual role demands executive workflow design, board preparation, and risk management.
- Performance evaluations that miss the mark.
- Compensation structures tied to a version of the role that no longer exists.
- Career ladders that stall or disappear because the position is misunderstood as static rather than a force of continuous impact.

I will always remember a role where I handled everything from board preparation to investor relations and cross-functional projects, yet I was still labeled as "admin support" in meetings I had organized. My leader, who often praised my contributions, once remarked that executive assistants were overpaid and questioned whether our salaries were justified.

Recognition and bias existed side by side.

That is what misalignment looks like: a disconnect between what is written on paper and what is happening day by day. And while it is rarely malicious, the consequences are the same: lack of recognition, unrealistic expectations, unfair pay, and systemic undervaluation.

The role has outgrown its one and only title. And it is time the world caught up.

Section 3 - The Cost: Underutilized Talent = Hidden Losses

When Executive Assistants are misjudged as "too junior" to contribute upstream, they are systematically underutilized. Their ideas get sidelined, their contributions go unseen, and the ripple effects are felt across the organization.

At best, there is confusion. At worst, neglect becomes baked into the system. And everyone pays the price.

Here is what happens when titles and scope do not align:

Leaders become bottlenecks. Instead of delegating strategically, they hoard decisions and tasks. Burnout spreads, not just to them, but across their teams.

EAs leave. The smartest, most capable ones seek out environments where their speed, skill, and strategic insight are acknowledged and rewarded.

Organizations lose continuity. Institutional memory begins to vanish. Established systems weaken. Culture destabilizes. Momentum falters.

And the cost runs even deeper.

"I was asked to run point on a multimillion-dollar system implementation, but when my evaluation came, I was graded against whether I scheduled travel accurately. That is when I knew the system was broken."

Failing to utilize an EA means forfeiting your most precious resource: time.

It means forfeiting trust, continuity, and risk protection. When an EA spots a looming issue but lacks the authority or credibility to be heard, organizations end up blindsided by problems that could have been avoided.

"I caught a compliance gap before it escalated to the board. But because I did not have the title or the voice in the room, leadership brushed it off. Six months later, it cost the company millions in fines."

Sometimes the misalignment is so glaring you cannot help but call it out. I remember sitting across from another EA describing her role. She was managing board communications, investor relations, and all executive workflows. As she spoke, I thought to myself, "this is a different universe than the role I just heard another EA describe in the same company."

One was strategic partnership at the highest level. The other was answering phones and ordering office supplies. Yet both held the exact same title.

This is the danger of mislabeling.

Another moment stands out vividly. I was introduced at a leadership meeting as "the admin support." In that same meeting, I presented the entire implementation plan for a multi-million-dollar system upgrade. The room froze. People did not know whether to treat me as a voice of authority or as someone who should fetch the coffee. That split second, that moment of mislabeling completely shifted how my contributions were received. The work did not change, but the perception of it did.

Mislabeling Leads to Mismanagement

Mislabeling Executive Assistants leads not only to miscommunication about their role but also to mismanagement of it. The way a role is defined influences funding, growth opportunities, promotions, and, crucially, the treatment of the individual in that position.

Leadership development opportunities disappear. Growth discussions come to a halt. Succession planning overlooks you, not due to a lack of ability, but because the title assigned does not represent the level at which you are already functioning.

Within the last decade, I worked in an organization where the only difference between an "Executive Assistant" and a "Senior Executive Assistant" was quite literally the title of the individual they supported. Not scope. Not decision-making authority. Not the complexity of the work. Just proximity to perceived power.

That is not a career ladder. That is not a competency model. That is hierarchy dressed up as structure.

And it is damaging because it does not just undermine the effectiveness of the EA. It misleads the entire organization.

It tells HR to pay based on title, not value. It tells leaders to allocate visibility based on assumption, not contribution. It reinforces a broken system that hides talent in plain sight.

The cycle is predictable. A lack of clarity leads to limited growth, which results in talent loss or stagnation, raising the question, why are we struggling to find good EAs these days?

The truth is, they were present all along. You just never noticed them completely.

"My executive told me I was the only person who truly kept him focused. Yet in the same breath, HR said I was not eligible for the leadership bonus pool. How can both things be true?"

Because the cost of sidelining strategic talent is not just organizational. It is personal. For high-level EAs, the calculation is constant: How long can I keep showing up for a role that refuses to see me?

"Eventually, you stop trying. You stop bringing the bigger ideas. And then you stop staying."

The answer is often: not long. And when they leave, what is lost is not just "support." What is lost is infrastructure, intelligence, and impact.

"The day I left, my executive said he was losing his right hand. But on paper, I was still listed as clerical staff. That disconnect is why I walked away."

The bottom line? Titles are not just labels. They signal worth, scope, and voice. And when we get them wrong, we risk misrepresenting brilliance as basic.

It is time to rewrite the narrative.

Chapter 3: The Job Description Teardown

Section 1: What We've Been Handed

I can't tell you how many Executive Assistant job descriptions I've read that felt like they were written in 1995 or later. It's like someone took a Microsoft Office template, added a line about "multitasking," and hit upload.

And if you've ever tried to explain the full scope of your work to a recruiter who's going off that outdated template, you already know the problem. You feel boxed in before you've even started. Your experience gets flattened into bullet points that say everything and nothing at the same time.

You can envision how this will transpire... you will be the "Department of Miscellaneous Tasks."

Let's break it down.

Here's what you'll usually see in a traditional EA job description:

- "Manage calendar and schedule meetings"
- "Coordinate travel arrangements"
- "Handle confidential information with discretion"
- "Act as a liaison between executive and team"

While technically accurate, it is severely lacking in detail. It resembles a task list for an automaton rather than a strategic ally engaged at the crossroads of leadership, logistics, and organizational insight.

And astonishingly, there are still some who use the term 'secretary.'

There's absolutely nothing wrong with being a secretary.

That role is not only important but also holds its own distinct place in the workplace. However, let's stop pretending that the titles are interchangeable, as each position carries its own unique responsibilities and significance.

An Executive Assistant is not a secretary.

The nature of the work, the expectations that come with the role, and the strategic impact they have on an organization are fundamentally different and much more complex.

This is fundamentally about systems and their implications. When HR, leadership, and entire industries categorize all administrative roles into one outdated bucket without differentiation, it sets off a ripple effect that leads to misrepresentation, underutilization, and significant undervaluation of these crucial positions.

It's time to call it.

This profession is filled with influential voices, immense intelligence, and significant impact. We cannot continue with the same old approaches. The outdated language is ineffective and hinders the progress of careers, teams, and organizations that have the potential to elevate their performance.

This isn't a gentle nudge. It's a teardown. And it starts here.

Section 2: Building, Not Minimizing, The Modern EA Role

If the previous job descriptions limit us, this section focuses on expanding our roles.

Let's stop trying to fit strategic minds into administrative templates. Let's stop defining modern EA roles by what we used to be and start designing them based on what we do.

We're not here to tweak a few bullet points. We're here to construct a new blueprint.

Here's what that looks like in real life:

- Instead of "Manage executive calendar" → "Own time architecture and decision flow across leadership priorities. manage up, across, and through changing operational demands."
- Instead of "Coordinate travel" → "Design and oversee logistical execution for executive mobility, including stakeholder access, travel ROI, and pre/post-movement alignment."
- Instead of "Liaison with internal teams" → "Function as the executive proxy and connective tissue across verticals, ensuring clarity, accountability, and momentum throughout execution."

These are not merely superficial adjustments. They signify a significant shift in perspective, transitioning from a reactive approach to support toward a more proactive stance focused on empowerment within leadership.

It's time to stop minimizing the role in our own language. What we build into the job description becomes the lens through which others interpret our value, our authority, and our future in the organization.

The updated job description isn't exaggerated; it's refined. It elevates the language to reflect the level of impact we're already achieving.

Section 3: Co-Creating the Future: It's Not Just an Admin Problem.

The reality is that the misrepresentation of the Executive Assistant role is not solely an issue for EAs to address.

HR cannot resolve this itself. Leaders cannot resolve this by themselves. And assistants should not be the only ones shouldering the responsibility of redefining it.

For this role to evolve, we must come together for a shared understanding and work collaboratively to redefine it.

Many executives have either never experienced having an effective executive assistant or are unaware of when they did. They lack exposure to the potential that can be achieved with the right person in that position, someone who is empowered and aligned with their goals.

As a result, their expectations are shaped by outdated models, ingrained habits, and simplistic organizational structures.

Some HR teams are constrained by job description libraries that are over ten years old. They depend on outdated language and past practices instead of considering, "What are the actual requirements for this role in today's environment?"

And the assistants?

We've been quietly filling those gaps, without the credit, clarity, or compensation that should come with it. So how do we change it?

We bring all three parties to the table.

Not symbolically. Not after the fact. From the start.

A Modern Job Description Process Should Include:

1. The Executive Assistant — who articulates the challenges of scope, speed, personnel, and pressure in a manner that no HR team can match.
2. The Executive — who grasps the strategic outputs and support occurring behind the scenes, frequently thanks to the Executive Assistant.
3. The HR Partner — who converts both perspectives into fair language that aligns with compensation frameworks and career progression paths.

Anything below is merely a rebranded misalignment.

Why This Matters More Than Ever?

- When a role is misdescribed, it is misperceived,
- When it's misperceived, it is mismeasured.
- And when it's mismeasured, it is underleveraged and undervalued, from day one.

To help your EAs develop alongside the company, you need to provide them with language that aligns with their actual roles.

Cultural Shift: What Co-Creation Signals

When you invite an EA into the process of defining their own role, you're not just clarifying expectations, you're acknowledging that role is worth designing well.

That's what we need more of.

- Not recycled templates.
- Not assumptions from the top down.
- Not oversimplified listings that sound like every other admin posting.

We need language that fits the weight of the work.

And we need more leaders brave enough to say, "Let's write it together."

This is the point where the change starts. Everything prior to this has been the reason.

This is the approach. It begins not with the Executive Assistant, but with the individuals and systems that support them.

The executive assistant understands their value. They can articulate their contributions. They manage three levels of responsibility that often go unnoticed. However, if HR fails to acknowledge this, if leadership does not recognize it, and if the necessary support structures are absent, their efforts will not be recognized.

That is the core problem in this situation.

HR: You are the system

Let's acknowledge that this goes beyond merely discussing leadership development.

- You write the detailed job codes that define roles.
- You benchmark and analyze the salaries to ensure fairness and competitiveness.
- You define the various career ladders to provide clear paths for advancement.
- You carefully frame the succession planning to prepare for future leadership needs.
- You shape and influence what is perceived as a truly legitimate and meaningful role within the organization.

If your EA job descriptions are outdated, if your leveling framework has no tiering for strategic EA work, if your title structure maxes out at "Senior Assistant" … You are not contributing to the business on a larger scale.

And that's not an exaggeration.

- In organizations that effectively scale and grow, the Executive Assistant function is perceived as a significant source of operational leverage and efficiency.
- In organizations that stagnate, EAs often find themselves boxed into a limited role focused on clerical service.

HR Audit Kit Breakdown: Real Change Starts Here

EA Role Scope Interview Template

Inquire with the EA about their actual responsibilities rather than relying on the job description.

To truly grasp the extent of an Executive Assistant's influence, it's essential to look beyond the job description. Titles alone do not capture the complete picture, nor do old bullet points from previous reorganizations.

Instead, pose inquiries that reveal what's truly occurring behind the scenes.

Inquiries such as:

- "What do you manage that no one else even knows exists?"
- "What systems stay functional because of your unspoken effort?"
- "If you walked away for a week, what would fall through the cracks?"
- "Where are you quietly making decisions that shape outcomes?"
- "What part of your job is invisible, but absolutely essential?"

These questions reveal the hidden work, the intricate management, and the significant oversight involved. They highlight the subtleties. Once acknowledged, it becomes much more difficult to downplay or ignore it.

HR, it is critical to refrain from requesting a bullet-point update on a job description. Instead, let's schedule a 30-minute discussion. This approach shows respect and will lead to valuable insights.

What is Measured is Valued

Let us stop here and talk about solutions. For Executive Assistants to be acknowledged for their contributions, we require more than mere recognition; we need a structured framework. This should be a concrete tool that both EAs and organizations can utilize to measure impact, rather than simply relying on the assumption that it is occurring.

Strategic Administrative Professional Matrix:

Action	Strategic Outcome	Organizational Value
Managed complex executive calendar	Protected decision-making capacity	Enables improved executive prioritization and output
Streamlined team operations during leadership transition	Maintained operational continuity	Prevented costly misalignment and loss of trust
Partnered in board prep, including content review	Sharped message clarity for key stakeholders	Elevated perception and trust in leadership

This is not theoretical.

This is how we translate the EA role into the language of outcomes, not outputs. It also gives EAs the language to describe their work in ways leadership can measure, elevate, and defend.

- We're not just "getting it done."
- We're driving clarity.
- We're reducing risk.
- We're increasing executive capacity.

Title Tier Sample Framework

We require specific titles rather than minimal vague ones. What we need is a well-defined and purposeful career progression.

The issue goes beyond the ambiguity of the title "Executive Assistant." It's being utilized as a catch-all for roles ranging from basic task support to complex executive management.

This situation is not only confusing but also unfair. We don't need another broad umbrella that tries to fit everyone.

Why this matters:

- It creates visibility into role evolution, from tactical execution to operational command to strategic partnership.
- It gives HR a structure for compensation that reflects scope, not assumptions.
- It equips leadership with clarity: where their EA is today, and where that partnership could grow.

If someone is managing board relations, serving as a proxy in leadership meetings, or stewarding executive priorities across departments, "assistant" is not only inaccurate, but also reductive.

This is about aligning titles with reality.

Progression Paths for the Modern EA

Band Level	Title Examples	Scope and Function
IC Level 1–2	Admin Assistant, Receptionist	Entry-level; task-driven, procedural, support-focused
IC Level 3	Executive Assistant (Traditional)	Calendars, travel, expenses; mostly reactive, low complexity
IC Level 4	Senior EA, Department Coordinator	Adds light ops, recurring reporting, vendor coordination, and minor project work
IC Level 5	Project Coordinator, Business Admin	Begins influencing systems; owns initiatives; partners more closely with leaders.
IC Level 6	Executive Business Partner	Manages cross-functional work; high discretion; owns communication + priorities
IC Level 7	Executive Integrator, Junior Chief of Staff	Owns workflows, org rhythms, stakeholder navigation; strategy meets structure
Director Tier	Chief of Staff, Head of Operations	Company-wide responsibility; executive proxy; leadership rhythm and decision cadence, Special Projects

So much of the EA title conversation comes down to one thing: truth.

- The truth of the scope.
- The truth of the impact.
- The truth of the role.

If we keep defining Executive Assistants by outdated templates and tired assumptions, we are not just minimizing the people doing the work, we are misrepresenting how business runs.

Realignment Process Checklist

This is precisely where many companies tend to drop the ball. They are aware that the scope of the Executive Assistant role has shifted significantly, but unfortunately, the organizational structure has not adapted to keep pace with these changes.

Here's an effective way to change that:
1. Audit EA roles organization wide.
2. Conduct real scope interviews.
3. Compare to current titles and JDs.
4. Draft updates with the EA and executive.
5. Review in HR/Leadership sync.
6. Implement org-wide updates (title, JD, pay band).
7. Communicate clearly and positively.
8. Follow up at 3–6 months.

HR Advice: Incorporate this into your quarterly workforce planning review instead of only addressing it through reactive promotions. When this is integrated, misalignment will become an exception rather than the standard.

The Role Realignment Loop

A continuous, 5-step cycle to keep EA scope, title, and compensation in sync.
Educate Leadership + HR → Review Quarterly + Repeat

1. Interview for Actual Scope
2. Update Job Description
3. Reassess Title + Compensation
4. Educate Leadership + HR
5. Review Quarterly + Repeat

Realignment isn't a one-time fix — it's a system shift.

Language Shapes Leverage

Let's get one thing straight: job descriptions aren't just internal documents.

- They're currency.
- They're negotiation tools.
- They're comp benchmarks.
- They shape first impressions, internal perceptions, and external recruitment.

When the words are wrong, the system misfires. This is not about ego, it is about infrastructure. The question is simple: what shifts when we stop documenting tasks and start defining impact?

Before and After Examples

Old JD Language	Modern JD Rewrite
Manage executive's calendar and schedule meetings	Architect executive time flow across enterprise priorities; optimize leadership rhythm and stakeholder alignment
Coordinate travel arrangements	Design and manage executive mobility strategies with ROI alignment and logistical precision
Answer calls and triage email	Protect executive signal integrity across all incoming channels; ensure high-value focus
Prepare meeting materials	Develop and curate strategic briefings that drive clarity and decision-making in real-time
Assist with special projects	Own cross-functional initiatives that advance business goals and eliminate friction

This isn't fluff. It's signal clarity.

- These rewrites tell a recruiter: this person isn't here to follow, they're here to drive.
- They tell HR: this is not a plug-and-play admin role, this is leadership enablement.
- They tell a candidate: you'll be seen, empowered, and compensated accordingly.

Strategic Impact: Language Drives Leveling.

What's written sets the ceiling—or removes it. Language impacts perception. If it sounds tactical, it will be treated that way.

Language sets the tone for growth. You don't scale talent on outdated templates.

Because what's written in a job description becomes the foundation for:

- How the role is valued
- How performance is measured
- How compensation is set
- How potential is either elevated or ignored

It's language. It's infrastructure. And if that foundation is built on outdated language, everything that follows will be misaligned.

ROI of Realignment

HR leaders and CFOs need to recognize that realignment is not just a superficial effort. It is not driven by surface-level concerns, or an acquiescence to title inflation. Instead, it is a strategic approach aimed at enhancing business performance.

Misalignment in the Executive Assistant role regarding title, compensation, and responsibilities can lead to disengagement and threaten operations, leadership stability, and institutional knowledge.

Attrition isn't just expensive. It's disruptive.

Beyond just the expense of finding a replacement, consider the value of what is lost:

- The time it takes to rebuild trust with an executive.

- The months spent re-mapping critical workflows.
- The drop in productivity as onboarding lags behind reality.

The harsh reality is that many companies fail to understand the level of value that person brought until they're no longer there. It's not until things start to slip, until follow-ups are missed, until meeting preparations become chaotic, and until the flow is disrupted that this becomes clear.

So yes, title alignment matters. So does pay equity.

And so does naming the scope with the respect it deserves.

The Hidden Cost of Misalignment: A Numbers View

When leaders underutilize or mislabel Executive Assistants, the impact is not only cultural but financial. Let's put it in terms organizations can measure:

- EA Salary (market average): $90,000
- Replacement Cost (average 1.5x salary for turnover): $135,000
- Misalignment Attrition (2 departures per year is common in high-turnover orgs): $270,000 annually

And that is only direct attrition cost. It does not factor in:
- Lost continuity during onboarding (slowed decision-making, missed context).
- Institutional knowledge walking out the door.
- The executive's time spent covering gaps instead of leading.
- The drag on morale and team stability.

Put simply: misalignment compounds. The organization pays in turnover, in hidden opportunity costs, and in diminished executive capacity.

As one EA put it:

"I left because the title kept me invisible. By the time they replaced me, it cost them twice my salary and six months of momentum. That was avoidable."

Add executive inefficiency, cultural friction, onboarding cost, and morale impact? You're easily losing half a million dollars a year.
And that doesn't even consider the burnout of the EA who remained but mentally disengaged.

Realignment pays for itself. Always.

Stop asking EAs to prove their worth. That's the takeaway.

Right there. If you take nothing else from this chapter, take that.

Stop putting the burden on Executive Assistants to justify their evolution. To document every extra responsibility, every strategic pivot, every way they've outgrown the outdated title that's still stapled to their HR file.

Don't ask them to build their own job description from scratch, just to be seen.

Don't ask them to write a case for why they're doing more, just to be considered for a reclass next year.

That's not strategy.

That's avoidance.

Instead, HR needs to ask this:

- What system allowed this much misalignment to go unchecked?
- What behaviors normalized the gap between what's written and what's required?

Because the EA didn't go rogue.

- They didn't inflate their value or step outside their lane.
- They evolved with the business.
- They adapted, with the executive(s).
- They scaled, with the organization's growing needs.

And the organization? It didn't keep up.

So now? The responsibility does not fall with the EA to justify the essential updates to their title, career progression, growth opportunities, and adjusted pay scales.

It is HR's duty, the culture shaper, to address what is no longer relevant.

Don't ask someone to justify the impact you've already relied on.

That's not just lazy, it's a leadership failure.

Chapter 4: Rewrite the Narrative

The voice that defines you shouldn't be borrowed or broken.

Section 1: Stop Shrinking the Role

Shrink the narrative, and the world will shrink your value. Own it, or others will define it for you. No recruiter, no org chart shift, no title change will rewrite the narrative unless we do.

Discretion over definition. Deference over decision-making. Invisibility over influence.

We were acknowledged for being those who could handle everything quietly, without resistance, and without requiring a title that reflected the responsibility we bore.

Adaptation isn't the same as alignment. And staying silent in the face of misalignment isn't humility, it's erosion. If you want the world to see the full scope of what you do, you must stop shrinking to fit inside a title that was never built to hold your capacity.

You don't require approval. You require accuracy. You need words that convey your influence, not just your role. You require a career ladder that clearly outlines opportunities for advancement. And you must stop wondering if it's too audacious to speak it openly.

Let's call it what it really was: Survival inside a structure that refused to evolve.

I've over-delivered in silence. I've cleaned up behind-the-scenes chaos that no one ever saw. I've watched leaders succeed while my own title stayed flat, my compensation stagnant, my work misunderstood.

And I told myself it was just part of the job. But here's the shift, here's the truth: We cannot let "how it's always been" be the voice in our heads anymore.

That voice—the one that whispers, "Be thankful just to be here," "You shouldn't take the lead," and "Don't seek more, just be content to support quietly"—is outdated. It harks back to an era when assistants were viewed as mere subordinates instead of strategic partners. It has no place in your career now. It's time to silence it.

As we continue to hold onto that mindset, we remain in positions that do not align with our true circumstances. This prolonged thinking allows companies to avoid meaningful discussions regarding responsibilities, job titles, career progression, and compensation.

The more we cling to this belief, the more we blur the line between humility and invisibility.

You were never meant to be invisible.

- You were intended to guide from your current position.
- To maintain standards.
- To foresee potential issues.
- To facilitate progress.
- To address shortcomings.
- To propel forward movement.

This is not work that goes unnoticed. This is executive leadership, carried out collaboratively.

We cannot change perception if we continue to undersell our work. We cannot build credibility by keeping our impact quiet.

We cannot expect respect if we're still introducing ourselves as "just" anything.

We must get out of the habit of playing small, especially when our impact is anything but.

Section 2: The Narrative We Carry

This section isn't about surface-level fixes. It's about doing the hard internal work of separating your identity from the outdated narratives that have followed this profession for decades.

Those narratives didn't appear by accident.

They were built into the very architecture of corporate life, cemented into policy, culture, language, and leadership structures long before any of us ever sat down at our desks. And I know that not because I read it in a white paper, but because I lived it. I've been a participant in this dynamic for more than 20 years. Not just a witness, but a player.

I've stayed quiet when I should've asked for clarity. I've accepted titles that didn't match my scope. I've swallowed moments of deep misalignment because I didn't want to seem "ungrateful." I've said yes when I should have set a boundary. I've taken pride in being invisible, indispensable, and impossibly efficient, even when it cost me clarity, compensation, or dignity.

 Why? Because like many of us, I was taught, through direct feedback or quiet cultural pressure, that:

Humility meant silence. Support meant servitude. Excellence meant invisibility.

And boundaries were barriers to being seen as a team player. And they still are!

We weren't just encouraged to stay behind the scenes; we were rewarded for it. Even when we were the ones holding the show together backstage.

I'm done with that.

- I've taken on the role of being "constantly available."
- I've put in long hours and have wondered if I was really providing value.
- I've agreed to things when I needed to say no,
- I've downplayed my contributions because I realized others were already doing the same, and I felt like I would be speaking a language no one else understood.

And if you've done that too, I see you. I really do.

It's not a flaw. It's how many of us learned to navigate survival.

But the reality is this, you can't create strength from a position of being unseen.

It took time, and a lot of unlearning, a lot of getting in my own way, or being "too nice," to start seeing myself as more than just the glue holding things together.

And even now, I must remind myself that rewriting the narrative isn't a switch you flip. It's practice. A muscle. One that requires daily intention.

Begin by allowing yourself to acknowledge the true significance of your work. It begins with recognizing how your role has changed, how you have developed in your career, and how both your mindset and personal narrative need to adapt accordingly.

It begins by posing a specific series of questions to yourself:

- Am I shrinking to protect someone else's comfort? Am I using humility as a disguise for fear?
- Am I calling something "teamwork" when it's scope creep?

This section is your invitation to reflect on the stories you've inherited, about worth, visibility, leadership, and what it means to support someone else.

You don't have to carry them forward. You get to write new ones.

And this time, you get to do it on your own terms.

Voices from the Chair

Maya | Technology Sector | 9+ Years in Executive Support
"I Had to Stop Being Reasonable"

I used to think if I just stayed reasonable, everything would eventually align, title, scope, pay, all of it.

So, I stayed late. I filled the gaps. I coached new leaders quietly and ran operations during three back-to-back leadership transitions. I didn't ask for more because I assumed the work would speak for itself.

But what I didn't realize was: the work can't speak if no one is listening.

When I finally asked for a scope adjustment and a title that matched what I was doing, the response was:

"You've just always handled it. We didn't know it had gotten that complex." That moment broke something — not in a bitter way, but in a truly obvious way.

I had let invisibility become part of my identity. I'd been waiting for someone else to validate the complexity of what I carried.

That's not happening again. Now, I document everything. I lead with clarity. I correct mislabels in real time, respectfully, but immediately.

I had to stop being reasonable in a system that didn't make reasonable room for my growth.

Danielle | Healthcare Sector | 15+ Years in Executive Support "From Supporting Role to Strategic Force"

What would surprise most people about my job scope is how far my role has evolved beyond the original job description. I began in a traditional, and often invisible, executive support capacity. But over time, I absorbed responsibilities left behind by both a former Assistant Vice President and a former Clinical Director, neither of whom were replaced.

Today, I'm still providing high-level executive support, but I'm also managing projects, leading programs, supervising staff, and driving cross-functional initiatives. I'm making strategic decisions and operating in spaces typically reserved for leadership titles, without the title or compensation to reflect it.

And yet, the work is real. The growth is undeniable. And the impact? It speaks for itself.

James | Financial Industry | 12+ Years in Executive Support   "I Didn't Get the Promotion, Just the Responsibility"

I was hired to manage one executive's calendar. But repeatedly, when senior managers left, their responsibilities landed on my desk. No backfill. No transition plan. Just quiet absorption.

Now, I'm overseeing investor reporting cycles, managing operational workflows across departments, leading project execution, and acting as a sounding board for strategic decisions. I've become the glue between departments, often the one bringing clarity when others are spinning.

Reflection Prompts

1. **Reflect on the last time someone misinterpreted what you do based solely on your job title.**
   - Did that misunderstanding impact the tone and direction of the conversation in any way?
   - Did it alter the level of access you were granted during that interaction?
   - Furthermore, did it shift your own perception of your worth and contributions?

2. **Executive Assistants:**
   - What is one internal story you're still believing about what it means to support someone else?
   - Who benefits when you stay quiet? And who suffers?
   - What do you need to unlearn before you can fully step into your value?

3. **Does your current job description reflect the reality of your work, or a fraction of it?**
   - If someone brand new reads it, what would they miss about your scope and strategic value?
   - If you could rewrite just one section, what would it say?

4. **When was the last time your job description was updated?**
    - Who participated in writing it, and who should've been?
    - What's one phrase that needs to go, and one that absolutely belongs?

5. **To every Executive Assistant:**

    You never needed permission to grow. You needed someone who saw your full capacity and had the clarity and courage to lead you as if it mattered.

    HR and Leadership—ask yourself:
    - Are we investing in the roles closest to leadership?
    - Are we earning trust—or just assuming it?
    - Are we guiding those who guide without ego?

Chapter 5: Leadership Makes or Breaks the Role

Section I: The Hard Truth Behind Exit Interviews

There are a couple names that come to mind when I think about what great leadership feels like.

Leaders who had ambitious standards but never led with fear.

Leaders who were decisive, but deeply human.

The kind who could hold you accountable and still make you feel supported.

Interestingly, both experiences took place in some of the most chaotic work settings I've encountered. This applies to the leaders I'm referring to as well! The stakes were elevated, the pressure unyielding, yet their leadership was remarkable not only for its resilience but also for its stability.

 Their presence didn't contribute to the disorder; it provided clarity.

I have been fortunate to work with these individuals in various roles and capacities, and my respect for them has only grown over time.

Both moved on to more fulfilling paths, but the impact they made during their tenure left a lasting imprint on me. I hold them in the highest regard, not only for their courage and confidence in setting clear expectations, but for their deep empathy toward employees, even when those employees didn't fully understand the reasons behind the decisions being made.

They were the kind of leaders who earned followership, not just compliance.

The comment, "They don't leave companies. They leave leaders," came straight from one of the only executives I've worked with who had the clarity and courage to say it aloud. And mean it.

This chapter is not addressed to Executive Assistants; it focuses on the individuals who guide them.

It is for HR.

 It is for department heads.

It is for founders, division leaders, C-suite executives, Chiefs of Staff, and yes, even the EAs who are starting to lead from where they sit and want to do it better.

If you oversee, work alongside, assess, depend on, or influence the career trajectory of an Executive Assistant, you are a leader. Your presence and actions are more impactful than you may think.

This chapter explores the real reasons people leave, the quiet damage of unchecked leadership, and the subtle power Executive Assistants have in influencing, and surviving, those dynamics. Because culture isn't a mission statement.

Culture is who gets promoted, who gets listened to, and who gets left behind.

And if you're reading this, you're likely in a position to shape that culture, or repair the damage it's already done.

Section 2: The Myth of the "Disposable Employee"

We've all seen the headlines: The Great Resignation. The Great Reshuffle. The Big Quit. Corporate think tanks and HR panels pointed to burnout, shifting generations, demands for flexibility, or preferences for remote work. While those factors played a role, they only scratched the surface.

The deeper truth is this: the wave of departures wasn't about where people wanted to work. It was about refusing to work for leaders and organizations that treated them as replaceable.

Employees are not disposable. When people feel neglected, minimized, or unsafe, no perk or policy can retain them. What companies dismiss as turnover is often the direct result of treating people like parts to be swapped out rather than partners to be valued. And no role illustrates this more clearly than the Executive Assistant. Organizations rely on EAs as the connective tissue of leadership, the carriers of continuity, and the keepers of institutional trust, yet too often, the title itself reduces them to something expendable. The so-called "resignation crisis" was not about employees walking away from work. It was about walking away from being treated as disposable.

People don't leave solely for higher pay; they seek greater purpose, and that sense of purpose often diminishes when leadership prioritizes appearances over genuine connection.

Certain organizations attempted to address the resignation crisis through reactive strategies like pizza parties, mental health webinars, and "stay interviews."

However, these initiatives completely missed the mark.

What retains employees is not the culture deck showcased on your website, but rather the daily interactions with their direct supervisor.

Are they respected? Do they feel trusted?

Are they included in decision-making or simply managed into silence?

The Great Resignation was never a workforce problem. It was, and still is, a leadership problem. At its core, it exposed the myth of the disposable employee. Until organizations confront this truth, that every role, including support and administrative, carries weight and value, then real retention will remain impossible."

They exclude. They withhold. They sideline people from meetings and projects, not for the good of the business, but to protect their own ego.

This kind of silent sabotage is one of the most dangerous and damaging forms of leadership failure, and one of the hardest to name.

It's a passive-aggressive method of elimination that spares the leader from direct conflict, but leaves the employee isolated, confused, and erased. And it happens far more than most organizations want to admit.

When someone is quietly pushed out rather than supported or coached or respectfully guided toward a better-fitting role with dignity and intention, the issue is rarely just performance.

It is frequently the outcome of a transactional leader, someone who only appreciates individuals when they fulfill an immediate requirement.

I have experienced this, as I'm certain many of you have too.

I was silenced by someone who lacked the courage to communicate honestly, to collaborate effectively, or to address the true issues in our partnership.

That experience hurt deeply, not because I felt undervalued, but because they didn't respect their own responsibility enough to lead with clarity.

They repeatedly avoided accountability by placing the full weight of problems on me, without ever pausing to examine their own contribution to the dynamic.

That isn't leadership. That's evasion.

Leadership means having hard conversations. It means taking the time to develop real plans, self-reflect, offer honest feedback, and uphold mutual accountability. It means standing in the discomfort long enough to do what's right, not just what's easy.

Section 3: What Drives Talent Away?

Organizations frequently rush to understand why talented individuals depart. They examine exit interview feedback, point fingers at the job market, or presume it's related to pay. However, what is seldom openly recognized is that the true reason people choose to leave is often emotional rather than logistical. It revolves around their feelings regarding the leadership to whom they answer.

People leave when they feel:

- Unseen
- Undervalued
- Undermined
- Or simply… unwelcome

This isn't limited to any one level or title. It happens to frontline workers, senior managers, and yes, Executive Assistants.

Especially Executive Assistants.

Administrative Professionals are the first to absorb cultural dysfunction. We are the shock absorbers, the intermediaries, the silencers of chaos in the background. And when leadership fails, it doesn't just show up in boardroom decisions or public-facing culture, it shows up in how assistants are communicated with, excluded, minimized, or ignored. The slow erosion of trust and respect is often the true tipping point.

Lack of Recognition and Respect

When a person's contributions are marginalized or dismissed as unimportant, they start to doubt their worth. This is a common experience for executive assistants. You might be the silent steward facilitating meetings, proactively addressing executive needs, and handling challenges smoothly, but still find yourself introduced as "just support."

The importance of that language cannot be overstated. It diminishes the strategic value of the work.

When leaders and organizations do not recognize, measure, promote, and reward the value of the EA function, it sends a message that this role is non- essential and easily replaceable. Over time, this perception influences the culture and can quickly affect employee retention.

Poor Communication and Inconsistency

Few things are more destabilizing than unclear, reactive leadership. EAs are often the first to spot these patterns, when expectations shift without notice, when decisions get made in silos, when priorities change without explanation.

This puts us in impossible positions. We're expected to be mind-readers and miracle workers but left out of the very conversations that would empower us to deliver with precision.

And when we seek clarity? Too often, the response is defensiveness or deflection. That's not leadership. That's insecurity wrapped in authority.

Micromanagement or Abandonment

Poor leaders tend to swing between extremes. They either smother their team with micromanagement, questioning every decision, inserting themselves into tasks they don't understand, or they completely disengage, expecting others to sense their needs without any guidance.

Neither style builds trust. And for EAs, who thrive on clarity, rhythm, and collaboration, these extremes are draining. They force us into constant adaptation mode, never knowing if we're overstepping or underdelivering.

Misaligned Values and Ethics

When a company makes promises but fails to follow through, its values diminish.

This is particularly evident to EAs who are positioned at the crossroads of communication and action. We listen to the commitments made in staff meetings and witness the realities that unfold behind the curtain. The disparity between declared values and actual practices is where trust begins to falter.

Once trust is lost, no retention strategy can mend it.

The Growth Ceiling No One Talks About

"People leave when they no longer believe they can grow." It's a simple truth, but it's the one we avoid the most, especially when it comes to Executive Assistants.

This is where businesses, HR departments, and leadership at large miss the mark entirely. Too often, the EA role is treated as an endpoint, not a pathway. You're placed in a box labeled "administrative support" and expected to stay there, even as your skills outpace your title, your impact expands, and your insight deepens.

We become the unofficial catch-all, called upon to anchor everything, yet excluded from the structures that would keep us tethered. What about when we request salary raise? We're told we're too expensive. That we make more than our "titled" coworkers. That our worth is hard to justify on paper.

For every EA who's been told "you're doing too much," for everyone who's been left out of the room they organized, for everyone who's been quietly replaced by someone less skilled, but more compliant...

This is your reminder, it's not you.

It's the system.

And systems can be changed.

This is the beginning of that change.

Section 4: The Leadership Gap

The term "leadership gap" often comes up in discussions regarding succession planning or skill development. However, there is another, less talked about gap that is far more detrimental, present in every industry and organization. This discrepancy exists between "the principles leaders profess to support" and "their true actions." It is not just a theoretical concern; it has tangible consequences and can be significantly harmful, especially for Executive Assistants.

The Damage of Disconnect

We've all seen it. Leaders who talk about trust but micromanage every move. Leaders who claim to care about culture but tolerate toxicity because the numbers look good. Leaders who say they value feedback but never invite dissent, or worse, retaliate against it.

This gap creates confusion, erodes morale, and drives out high performers who can no longer reconcile the double standard.

It's especially acute for EAs, who are expected to model the leadership tone even when the executive does not. We're expected to make others feel heard when we're silent. To hold confidentiality while others violate trust. To be calm when chaos is self-inflicted by the very people in charge. That double standard is unsustainable.

The Emotional Toll

Living in this gap creates a type of invisible labor that rarely gets acknowledged.

- It's emotional buffering.
- It's relational maintenance.
- It's protecting the brand of a leader who hasn't earned the loyalty they're relying on.

It's being the culture, without being empowered to shape it. And it takes a toll. EAs in these environments often burn out, not because the tasks are hard, but because the values are hollow.

How Leadership Should Be Demonstrated

To move forward effectively, we not only must identify what is currently missing but also clearly define what our future is.

It is essential to draw a clear contrast between the two approaches:

- Transactional Leadership, which is what we do not need in our organizations, and
- Transformational Leadership, which is precisely what we need to foster growth and innovation.

Culture is what leaders tolerate, repeat, and model, especially when no one's watching.

- The voices that are listened to.
- The individuals that are overlooked.
- The employees that are promoted.
- The people that absorb the consequences.

If EAs are expected to perform at a leadership level, they must be supported at one too. And if leaders want loyalty, they must earn it, not assume it.

This is the leadership gap. And it's time to close it.

Transactional Leadership and EAs

- Task Delegation Only: Views the EA as a task-taker, not a strategic partner.
- Rigid Hierarchy: Reinforces outdated power structures and gatekeeping.
- Lack of Feedback Loop: Doesn't seek or value insight from EA despite proximity to operations.
- Short-Term Focus: Manages day-to-day logistics without considering long-term growth or capacity.
- Avoidance of Discomfort: Shies away from hard conversations, leaving issues unaddressed.
- Control over Collaboration: Prioritizes control rather than inviting EA input and shared leadership.
- Invisible Contribution: Fails to recognize or give credit for the EA's contributions or ownership. Provides no opportunities for development or progress.

This leadership style relies on control, not collaboration.

It limits the growth of everyone involved.

Transformational Leadership

- Strategic Partnership: Sees the EA as a trusted advisor, not just a support role.
- Mutual Respect: Operates with dignity, transparency, and shared humanity at every level.
- Two-Way Communication: Creates space for feedback, insight, and initiative-taking collaboration.
- Long-Term Vision: Builds systems with scalability, sustainability, and capacity in mind.
- Embraces Discomfort: Welcomes honest conversations and accountability for continuous growth.

- Shared Impact: Invites EA input and leverages influence, not hierarchy, to lead.
- Tangible Impact: Recognizes the EA's role in driving results and reinforcing culture through growth and advancement opportunities.

This leadership fosters capability, trust, and long-term commitment.

It encourages expansion.

Section 5: The Executive Assistant's Vantage Point

Few people in an organization have the vantage point of an Executive Assistant. EAs sit at the intersection of impact and process, watching everything from decision-making to damage control unfold in real time.

We know what was promised externally and what's possible internally.

We hold the pulse of people and the tempo of leadership, all while navigating our own invisibility.

This positions us as both observers and indicators. We frequently notice misalignments before they are apparent to the wider organization. We detect cultural changes before the official reorganization memo reaches inboxes. We are aware when morale declines, when negativity rises, and when leadership is more about appearances than genuine guidance.

When it's evident that change is necessary, we tend to be the first to recognize it.

Seeing Without Being Seen

It's common for EAs to quietly collect concerns from the team, field unspoken tensions, and function as a buffer between leadership and fallout. But that role has an emotional cost, especially when the very leaders we protect are unaware, or uninterested in, what we observe.

We turn chaos into clarity and urgency into calm—and still, we're treated as task support. That mismatch isn't just frustrating. It's exhausting.

A Role Built on Discretion

Part of what makes the EA role so powerful is also what makes it so easy to ignore: our discretion.

- We don't brag.
- We don't interrupt.
- We don't center ourselves.
- We lead through influence, not ego.

But that quiet strength is frequently mistaken for passivity. Our behind-the-scenes mastery becomes invisible labor. Our impact goes unspoken, until we're gone, and the gaps become undeniable.

We are the bond, the guide, the tranquility.

What They Don't Always See

Here's what high functioning EAs do and what leaders often miss:

- We safeguard their time, attention, and reputation daily. We set boundaries they struggle to maintain.

- We address issues before they reach their inbox, without seeking credit. We carry the emotional labor that leadership overlooks.
- We keep teams aligned, calendars strategic, and pressure manageable. We advocate for equity, even at a cost to our influence.

When we address toxic behavior, inadequate planning, misguided choices, or values that are out of sync with reality, we are not merely voicing complaints. We are highlighting weaknesses in the foundation before it collapses.

We are essential, not just an expense. We represent the strategic advantage that many leaders have yet to fully realize. However, this potential can be tapped into if they are open to recognizing it.

Section 6: Red Flags, Reframes & the Role of the EA Voice.

Highlighting what's wrong is not sufficient. True leadership involves recognizing when something is amiss and acting.

However, we must first understand what to identify. We require a vocabulary to describe the patterns and a means to differentiate between challenging times and detrimental leadership.

Red Flags We Should All Recognize

- Blame Without Reflection: When leaders assign blame without reflecting on their own role in an issue, it's not leadership; it's evasion. Every individual plays a part in results, including leaders. Particularly leaders.
- Exclusion as a Control Tactic: Removing people from meetings or loops without context or justification isn't

"streamlining." It's manipulation. Especially when it's done to avoid accountability or discomfort.

- Silencing Through Subtlety: When a person is removed without discussion, a chance to adjust, or clear feedback, the problem lies not in their performance but in the leader's unease with conflict.
- Reinforcing Hierarchy to Dismiss Input: When someone's concerns or insights are dismissed because of title, tenure, or perceived "place" in the hierarchy, it's a signal power, not truth, is driving the agenda.

Section 7: Leadership Is Culture, Not Just Command

We frequently encounter the saying "culture eats strategy for breakfast," yet we often overlook who shapes that culture from the start. It's not the HR team, the company's branding efforts, or the values displayed on the walls.

It comes down to leadership. Leadership defines culture because people reflect the behaviors of those in power.

When a leader takes shortcuts, others are likely to follow suit. If a leader shows humility in listening, others will too. Conversely, if a leader ignores concerns, manipulates feedback, or allows toxic behavior, the culture will mirror that. People aren't focused on the organizational chart; they pay attention to who receives recognition, who advances, and who is shielded.

The Assistant's View of Culture

EAs see these patterns faster than most.

We know which leaders operate with integrity, and which perform it. We notice who hoards information versus who shares freely.

We know who takes accountability, and who passes the blame.

We live at the crossroads of leadership intention and employee experience. Which means we're often the first to feel when something isn't right.

But here's the hard part: When we voice our opinions, we are frequently overlooked due to our position in the organizational hierarchy, and our titles do not hold significance. This is true even when we are the ones keeping everything intact.

How Culture Fails EAs

Culture deteriorates significantly when it prioritizes closeness to authority over meaningful contributions from its members. This decline is evident when executive assistants receive private commendations for their work but are consistently overlooked in public recognition or growth opportunities.

It becomes even more problematic when executive backing is treated as if it were merely administrative tasks, rather than being recognized as vital strategic support that is crucial for the organization's success and growth.

This double standard communicates a clear message: "We appreciate your results, but we refuse to acknowledge your contribution."

This is not only disheartening, but it also poses a risk. When assistants feel expendable, they become disengaged. And when they become disengaged, leaders forfeit their most essential support.

Fixing the Culture Starts with the Truth

This isn't merely an issue of support; it represents a significant leadership challenge. If leaders genuinely aspire to change the existing culture within their organizations, they must first start by examining their own behaviors and attitudes. Additionally, it is crucial to pay close attention to the executive assistants, as they have been reflecting on this culture all along and can provide valuable insights.

Section 8: It Was Never "Just" the Job

Retention isn't about rewards. It's not about snacks, swag, or even salaries alone. It's about whether people feel seen, supported, and safe to grow.

It is vital for organizations to acknowledge the significant impact Executive Assistants have, instead of seeing the position solely as one that manages calendars and arranges catering. We require the same level of clarity in our titles that 95% of career paths are afforded, along with access to educational and development opportunities.

Many assistants remain in their roles longer than they should due to loyalty to their leaders, teams, and a mission they once believed in. However, even the most resolute individuals will leave when they no longer feel a sense of trust or are inspired by growth.

When they decide to leave, it's seldom solely about the job itself.

If you want to retain great EAs, you must build systems that recognize their complexity. You must design partnerships that are rooted in mutual accountability, not silent service. And you must create environments where leadership is shared, not just performed at the top.

Because talent that is nurtured becomes foundational. Talent that is ignored becomes temporary.

"When Executive Assistants are empowered, they don't just support leadership. they elevate it. Stop minimizing the role and start recognizing the impact."

— Anne Browning

Chapter 6: Building the Future of Executive Assistants

Section 1: The Weight of History, and the Work It Ignores

The title of Executive Assistant has not developed in isolation. Its background is intricately linked to societal expectations regarding gender, hierarchy, and labor, particularly within Western corporate environments. Although the role has transformed, the terminology has remained static. Consequently, the title's ongoing association with antiquated notions often diminishes the professional authority and strategic influence of those who bear it.

Historically, the role of a personal or executive secretary, which would eventually evolve into what we now recognize as the modern-day Executive Assistant, was among the very first professional office positions accessible to women. These roles were inherently administrative by design, encompassing tasks such as typing, dictation, filing, and serving as a crucial liaison between the executive and everyone else in the organization.

When the term "assistant" was introduced as a more contemporary title, it unfortunately carried over the same historical baggage, often perceived as supportive, subordinate, and inherently gendered, reflecting long-standing stereotypes about women's roles in the workplace.

This evolution highlights the complex relationship between title and perception in the professional landscape.

The title still carries its history — and the bias baked into it.

And while titles like "manager," "partner," or "advisor" often signal expertise and leadership, "assistant" continues to suggest a backseat role, regardless of how central you are to the engine of the business.

But the work has changed. Dramatically.

A nuanced pattern emerges in high-level executive support roles, so nuanced that many overlook it. However, many of us are aware of it. We encounter it every day.

When you address a challenge effectively and with precision, without drawing attention to it, it suddenly becomes your responsibility. Not because it's your job. But because you're the one who can do it and do it well.

You begin to manage your superiors, then your peers, and even cross- functionally within the organization. You establish yourself as a reliable resource for others during times of uncertainty, instability, or sensitive political situations. I've lost track of how often I've navigated tough conversations and emerged successfully!

And over time, the boundaries blur.

You're not just managing calendars; you're filtering noise, identifying patterns, and making real-time decisions about what deserves your executive's time and what doesn't.

You're not just coordinating meetings; you're engineering outcomes, curating who's in the room, setting the pace, managing the energy, and ensuring that conversations translate into actions.

You're not just tracking tasks; you're steering the ship, aligning decisions to priorities, catching what others miss, and quietly shaping strategy from behind the scenes.

None of this is mentioned in a job description. Much of it remains unarticulated. However, that's the essence of this role at its peak; it's not about your actions, but about what you empower others to achieve.

And the danger?

Your ability to make everything appear effortless leads to it being overlooked. The unchanging title causes the extent of the work to be disregarded. And since it all unfolds quietly, the burden you bear stays hidden, until it suddenly isn't.

This is the established pattern. If we do not identify it, confront it, and reshape it, the responsibility to prove oneself will remain with those who are contributing the most. Yet, the designation remains "Executive Assistant." This is more than just a matter of terminology; it reflects a deeper issue of systemic framing.

When gender and hierarchy influence a title, it affects how individuals are treated, how their authority is recognized (or overlooked), and how their pay is decided. Additionally, there is a significant disconnect, a painful one, between the scope of work and how it is perceived, between actual contributions and the recognition they receive.

Section 2: Scope Creep, Role Drift, and the Executive Umbrella

A distinctive and challenging aspect of executive support is how responsibilities can subtly grow. You are entrusted with additional tasks, included in strategic discussions, and gain greater visibility. However, your title remains the same, your compensation does not increase, and the perception of your role does not evolve accordingly.

This phenomenon can be described as 'executive umbrella creep.'

Responsibilities that aren't explicitly assigned but are essential to the mission tend to fall to the executive assistant. Tasks like HR, communications, vendor management, event strategy, and operations, if they relate to the executive, they're placed under your purview. While this expansion of duties often signifies trust, it also creates a systemic issue.

When these additional responsibilities aren't acknowledged in your job title, description, or compensation, they become overlooked, even though they significantly shape your daily work.

In many fields, an expanded scope often leads to a new title: Coordinator evolves into Manager, and Manager advances to Director.

Not for executive support roles.

I once oversaw a comprehensive RFP process for a health system's records storage vendor. The board identified the issue and appointed my executive to spearhead the initiative, which effectively placed me in charge. I managed the internal project team, identified the vendor's shortcomings, explored other options, conducted interviews, performed due diligence, and implemented a system-wide solution that reduced legal risks and operational consequences.

My job description never mentioned I would be responsible for leading enterprise risk assessments and managing vendor transitions.

However, I accomplished those tasks successfully, with significant and system-wide positive outcomes, without receiving any significant recognition.

That's what the job required, even if the job description never mentioned it.

Section 3: The True Cost of Misalignment

Over time, your responsibilities and your job title can start to differ. What begins as a praise, "You're so talented, we can depend on you for additional tasks," can evolve into an unreasonable expectation. While your performance may enhance, the recognition may not keep pace.

That misalignment comes with a cost:

- Burnout: You're managing expanded responsibilities without increased authority or support.
- Under-compensation: Your pay is tied to a title that no longer reflects your actual role.
- Undervaluation: You're not included in leadership conversations because your title doesn't suggest you belong there.
- Turnover risk: High-functioning EAs leave, not because they can't manage the job, but because the job outgrew the support it receives.

The issue isn't about capacity; it's about clarity. Until the title aligns with the work, organizations will keep losing value where perception meets reality.

Section 4: Reframing the Narrative, Internally and Externally

If you are waiting for someone else to redefine your role, you will be waiting a long time. That is not pessimism. It is pattern recognition.

Many executives and HR teams do not intend to undervalue their EAs; they just haven't adjusted to the changes in the role. If you're looking for a signal to express your thoughts, consider this your go-ahead.

People often overlook the complexities involved in a process.

What appears to be a quick task may stem from weeks of preparation and intricate relationship management. If you remain silent, others might mistakenly think your work is simple or, even more concerning, insignificant. To be clear, your role doesn't require justification; it requires precise expression.

Parallel Role Journal

Follow the structure outlined below to record your entries over the next two weeks. Be sure to articulate what you enabled, protected, and/or prevented in a strategic way.

What I did	What I Enabled / Protected / Prevented
Coordinated a leadership offsite with 48 hours' notice	Prevented a $75K launch delay, reinforced executive alignment, and safeguarded stakeholder engagement.
Managed conflicting priorities across multiple departments	Protected executive capacity, minimized misalignment, and preserved team momentum.
Facilitated urgent board prep	Enabled timely decision-making and protected organizational credibility at the leadership level.

Conversation Starters

Use these to advocate for title and compensation alignment:
Opening lines:

- "My role has evolved in scope and complexity. Can we revisit how it is defined and recognized?"
- "The language around my title no longer matches what I am doing. Let us explore an update for clarity."
- "I've tracked my strategic contributions over the last month; can we review together how that aligns with compensation and scope?"

Final Reminder

Reframing is not inflating.

- It is translating.
- It protects your professional identity.
- It models clarity for the next generation.

Either you define your worth, or it will be defined in ways that keep you small.

~ Anne Browning ~

Section 5: The Work Deserves Better—And So Do We

We have been dancing around the truth of the Executive Assistant role for far too long. We have tried to elevate the work without changing the title. We have added responsibilities without revising compensation. We have celebrated EAs on social media while ignoring the outdated job descriptions collecting dust in HR systems.

It's not enough anymore. The work has evolved. The expectations have shifted. The value is undeniable. But the structure? The perception? The systems that surround it? They are stuck in the 1960s

Whether you're an EA, an HR professional, a department leader, or a C-suite executive, you are now part of the solution. Or you're choosing to stay part of the problem.

There is no middle ground.

If You Are a Leader of Any Kind

You can't claim your EA is "invaluable" while excluding them from important discussions. You can't commend their loyalty without providing opportunities for advancement. You can't refer to them as a "strategic partner" while approving a title that sounds like a junior admin position from the 1980s. This is a moment of reflection.

When your Executive Assistant curates your time, aligns your communications, orchestrates your priorities, and anticipates what's next, you are not merely supported, you are strengthened.

You are not leading alone. You are leading with a partner.

- Include EAs in discussions, from beginning to end. Acknowledge their contributions openly.
- Develop a career progression within this field.
- Support their title to align with their responsibilities. Involve them in succession planning, board preparation, cultural discussions, and the business strategies they are already assisting you with behind the scenes.
- Use your voice to elevate theirs.

If You Are in HR or People Operations

Look closely at your administrative titles. When was the last time they were reviewed? Do they reflect current responsibilities? Do they differentiate between tactical support and strategic partnership? If not, you're not just behind, you're complicit in underutilization, under compensation, and attrition.

It's not enough to say, "We couldn't do this without them."

- You must codify that in your systems.
- Build tiered progression ladders for executive support roles.
- Involve EAs in revising outdated job descriptions.
- Create benchmarks that reflect complexity, decision-making proximity, and enterprise visibility.
- Educate your leadership team on how to partner with EAs, not just assign tasks to them.

Do the work. Not because it's trendy. Because it's overdue.

If You Are an Executive Assistant

Stop waiting for permission to own the power of your work.

You know what you manage. You know how your support shapes outcomes. You know what falls apart when you're not there. And you are no longer required to justify the impact of your contributions in generic, watered-down language.

- Start naming what you do with precision.
- Start speaking about your work the way a Chief of Staff or Ops Partner would.
- Stop defaulting to "just," just the assistant, just planning, just support.

You're the linchpin. The integrator. The force that makes leadership functional.

Claim it. Without apology.

And if your organization won't recognize it? That is not yours to carry. It is a signal to assess whether your workplace is evolving—or simply holding on to the past.

This isn't Mad Men. Let's update the script.

This isn't a plea for favors. It's a push for accuracy. This isn't about nostalgia, it's about accuracy.

The Executive Assistant role has outgrown the stereotypes, the soft language, and the systems that keep it boxed in. Today's EAs are leading behind the scenes, operating at the heart of strategy, culture, and execution. The work is modern.

The stakes are higher.

And the title? It's overdue for a rewrite.

This is the time for us to change the dynamics.

- Let this year mark the end of labeling the role inaccurately.
- Let this year be when we establish the framework we have needed for decades.
- Let this be the year we stop minimizing, start defining, and lead with the clarity that this profession has always warranted.

The proof is already in the work.

It's the world that needs to catch up.

To every Executive Assistant, Administrative Partner, and Operations Professional

You are not invisible.

You are not "just support."

You are the infrastructure. You are the intelligence.

You are the force that drives organizations forward.

And Executive Assistant work demands more:

Title accuracy.

A career ladder that matches its scope.

A future that reflects its true power.

THE EXECUTIVE ASSISTANT MINIMIZING ENDS HERE. THE REDEFINING BEGINS NOW.

~ Anne Browning ~

Appendix: Resources

Reflection Prompts

Reflect on the last time someone misinterpreted what you do based solely on your job title.

- Did that misunderstanding impact the tone and direction of the conversation in any way?
- Did it alter the level of access you were granted during that interaction?
- Furthermore, did it shift your own perception of your worth and contributions?

Does your current job description reflect the reality of your work, or a fraction of it?

- If someone brand new reads it, what would they miss about your scope and strategic value?
- If you could rewrite just one section, what would it say?

When was the last time your job description was updated?

- Who participated in writing it, and who should've been?
- What's one phrase that needs to go, and one that absolutely belongs?

Executive Assistants:

- What is one internal story you're still believing about what it means to support someone else?
- Who benefits when you stay quiet? And who suffers?
- What do you need to unlearn before you can fully step into your value?

To every Executive Assistant:

You never needed permission to grow. You needed someone who saw your full capacity and had the clarity and courage to lead you as if it mattered.

HR and Leadership—ask yourself:

- Are we investing in the roles closest to leadership?
- Are we earning trust—or just assuming it?
- Are we guiding those who guide without ego?

EA Role Scope Interview Template

Inquire with the EA about their actual responsibilities rather than relying on the job description.

To truly grasp the extent of an Executive Assistant's influence, it's essential to look beyond the job description. Titles alone do not capture the complete picture, nor do old bullet points from previous reorganizations.

Instead, pose inquiries that reveal what's truly occurring behind the scenes.

Inquiries such as:

- "What do you manage that no one else even knows exists?"
- "What systems stay functional because of your unspoken effort?"
- "If you walked away for a week, what would fall through the cracks?"
- "Where are you quietly making decisions that shape outcomes?"
- "What part of your job is invisible, but absolutely essential?"

These questions reveal the hidden work, the intricate management, and the significant oversight involved. They highlight the subtleties.

Strategic Administrative Professional Matrix:

Action	Strategic Outcome	Organizational Value
Managed complex executive calendar	Protected decision-making capacity	Enables improved executive prioritization and output
Streamlined team operations during leadership transition	Maintained operational continuity	Prevented costly misalignment and loss of trust
Partnered in board prep, including content review	Sharped message clarity for key stakeholders	Elevated perception and trust in leadership

This is not theoretical.

This is how we translate the EA role into the language of outcomes, not outputs. It also gives EAs the language to describe their work in ways leadership can measure, elevate, and defend.

- We're not just "getting it done."
- We're driving clarity.
- We're reducing risk.
- We're increasing executive capacity.

Before and After Examples

Old JD Language	Modern JD Rewrite
Manage executive's calendar and schedule meetings	Architect executive time flow across enterprise priorities; optimize leadership rhythm and stakeholder alignment
Coordinate travel arrangements	Design and manage executive mobility strategies with ROI alignment and logistical precision
Answer calls and triage email	Protect executive signal integrity across all incoming channels; ensure high-value focus
Prepare meeting materials	Develop and curate strategic briefings that drive clarity and decision-making in real-time
Assist with special projects	Own cross-functional initiatives that advance business goals and eliminate friction

Parallel Role Journal

Follow the structure outlined below to record your entries over the next two weeks. Be sure to articulate what you enabled, protected, and/or prevented in a strategic way.

What I did	What I Enabled / Protected / Prevented
Coordinated a leadership offsite with 48 hours' notice	Prevented a $75K launch delay, reinforced executive alignment, and safeguarded stakeholder engagement.
Managed conflicting priorities across multiple departments	Protected executive capacity, minimized misalignment, and preserved team momentum.
Facilitated urgent board prep	Enabled timely decision-making and protected organizational credibility at the leadership level.

Progression Paths for the Modern EA

Band Level	Title Examples	Scope and Function
IC Level 1–2	Admin Assistant, Receptionist	Entry-level; task-driven, procedural, support-focused
IC Level 3	Executive Assistant (Traditional)	Calendars, travel, expenses; mostly reactive, low complexity
IC Level 4	Senior EA, Department Coordinator	Adds light ops, recurring reporting, vendor coordination, and minor project work
IC Level 5	Project Coordinator, Business Admin	Begins influencing systems; owns initiatives; partners more closely with leaders.
IC Level 6	Executive Business Partner	Manages cross-functional work; high discretion; owns communication + priorities
IC Level 7	Executive Integrator, Junior Chief of Staff	Owns workflows, org rhythms, stakeholder navigation; strategy meets structure
Director Tier	Chief of Staff, Head of Operations	Company-wide responsibility; executive proxy; leadership rhythm and decision cadence, Special Projects

So much of the EA title conversation comes down to one thing: truth.

- The truth of the scope.
- The truth of the impact.
- The truth of the role.

Realignment Process Checklist

This is precisely where many companies tend to drop the ball. They are aware that the scope of the Executive Assistant role has shifted significantly, but unfortunately, the organizational structure has not adapted to keep pace with these changes.

Here's an effective way to change that:
1. Audit EA roles organization wide.
2. Conduct real scope interviews.
3. Compare to current titles and JDs.
4. Draft updates with the EA and executive.
5. Review in HR/Leadership sync.
6. Implement org-wide updates (title, JD, pay band).
7. Communicate clearly and positively.
8. Follow up at 3–6 months.

HR Advice: Incorporate this into your quarterly workforce planning review instead of only addressing it through reactive promotions. When this is integrated, misalignment will become an exception rather than the standard.

The Role Realignment Loop

A continuous, 5-step cycle to keep EA scope, title, and compensation in sync.

Educate Leadership + HR → Review Quarterly + Repeat

6. Interview for Actual Scope
7. Update Job Description
8. Reassess Title + Compensation
9. Educate Leadership + HR
10. Review Quarterly + Repeat